Very EASY BORDERS by the Yard

by Nancy Smith & Lynda Milligan

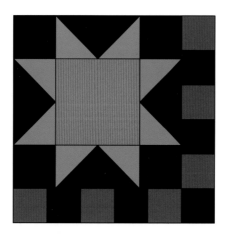

CREDITS

Sharon Holmes – Editor, Technical Illustrator
Lexie Foster – Cover, Designer, Graphics
Susan Johnson – Designer
Christine Scott – Editorial Assistant
Sandi Fruehling – Copy Reader
Brad Bartholomew – Photographer

THANKS

Ann Petersen, Jane Dumler – Information for General Directions
Ann Petersen, Jane Dumler, Katie Wells, Susan Auskaps, Courtenay Hughes – Sewing & Quilting

Every effort has been made to ensure that the information in this book is accurate. Due to individual skills, conditions, and tools, we cannot be responsible for any losses, injuries, or other damages that may result from its use.

…Fabric designers for AvLyn, Inc., publishers of DreamSpinners®
patterns & I'll Teach Myself™ & Possibilities® books…
Home of Great American Quilt Factory, Inc.

Very Easy Borders by the Yard
Published in the United States of America by Possibilities®, Denver, Colorado
ISBN: 1-880972-48-4

GENERAL DIRECTIONS

Borders & More is preprinted border yardage that can be used to decorate just about anything! Use it for quilt borders, sashing, and blocks. Add borders to purchased bedding such as sheets, pillowcases, and dust ruffles. Add border elements to throw pillows, wall hangings, valances, place mats, and tote bags.

Two repeats of each border across the yardage provide 12 border pieces in all, two of each pattern, with ¼" seam allowance included on all pieces.

Calculating how much to buy is easy. For quilt borders, buy a piece that is slightly longer than the width plus the length of your quilt. For double-gathered or pleated dust ruffles or valances, purchase yardage equal to the finished length of the item after gathering or pleating.

For ease of use, yardage can be cut apart in the places shown below. Each border can then be rolled on a cardboard tube. This makes the borders ready to use, easy to store, and wrinkle free.

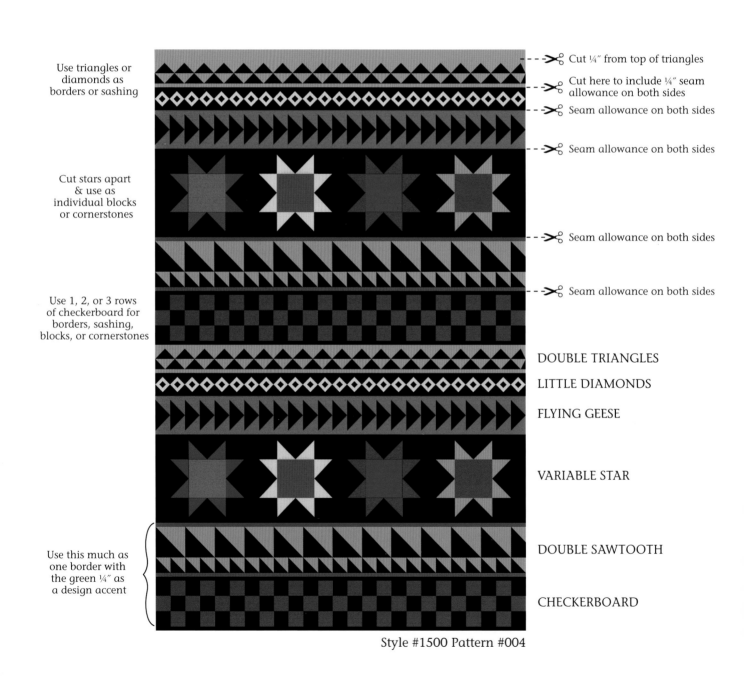

Use triangles or diamonds as borders or sashing

Cut stars apart & use as individual blocks or cornerstones

Use 1, 2, or 3 rows of checkerboard for borders, sashing, blocks, or cornerstones

Use this much as one border with the green ¼" as a design accent

Cut ¼" from top of triangles

Cut here to include ¼" seam allowance on both sides

Seam allowance on both sides

Seam allowance on both sides

Seam allowance on both sides

Seam allowance on both sides

DOUBLE TRIANGLES

LITTLE DIAMONDS

FLYING GEESE

VARIABLE STAR

DOUBLE SAWTOOTH

CHECKERBOARD

Style #1500 Pattern #004

We do not recommend prewashing Borders & More fabric.

SUGGESTIONS FOR USING BORDERS & MORE

STAIRSTEP CORNERS – Cut border pieces to fit the sides of the quilt and stitch them to the quilt. Then cut top and bottom borders to fit and stitch them to the quilt. This will result in the pattern crossing at the corner as shown.

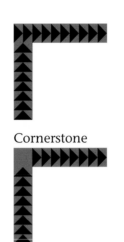

Cornerstone

CORNERSTONES – Cut a square of fabric the width of the border plus seam allowance and stitch it into the quilt at each corner.

DIVIDING DESIGN ELEMENTS – For a simple solution to making borders fit, center the design of a border from end to end and trim excess.

Divide the difference end to end

COPING STRIPS – Cut the border on a design element (adding ¼″ seam allowance) and then add a coping strip of a coordinating fabric to get the needed length.

Coping Strips

COPING BORDERS – Coping borders bring the size of a quilt up to a measurement which will match a whole design element in the printed border. All the design elements in **Borders & More** are based on 1″ or 2″, making it easy to adjust the size of a quilt with coping borders so each printed border will end with a complete design element. Coping borders are often different widths for the sides of the quilt versus the top and bottom. They may be as narrow as ¼″ or as wide as several inches.

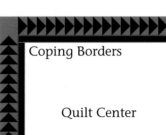

Coping Borders

Quilt Center

To figure the widths for coping borders, start by measuring the length of the well-pressed quilt center. Next, measure the length of the desired printed border, in full design elements. The border may end at the next full design element or be several elements longer. Subtract the length of the quilt center from the desired length of the printed border piece. Divide by two. This is the width of the top and bottom coping borders. Don't forget to add

seam allowance. Repeat with the width of the quilt to determine the width of the side coping borders. Use the same fabric as the background of the quilt center to make the center look as if it is floating, or choose a contrasting fabric to make the separation more obvious.

BLOCKS – Cut up Borders & More to make blocks. The stars and the checkerboard lend themselves most readily to this, but other borders may be used as elements in blocks also. See the quilt on page 4. Don't forget to add seam allowances when designing blocks. When borders are cut crosswise, a design element will be lost between pieces.

If the design elements are smaller than desired, enlarge the size of the block by adding strips of border fabric or another coordinating fabric to two sides or to four sides of the block.

Dotted lines indicate original elements

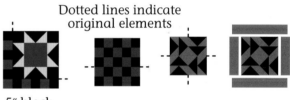

5″ block becomes 6″ block

SASHING – The narrower borders in the Borders & More yardage work well as sashing. Using cornerstones at the intersections simplifies the construction of the sashing and enhances many designs. Elements from the border can also be used as cornerstones with plain sashing strips.

Sashing Strips

Cornerstones

QUILTING – Quilting on the lines between design elements, similar to ditch quilting, makes the quilt look pieced.

HINT

When stitching printed borders to quilt center or blocks, put the border on top and stitch on the line.

SPRINKLING OF STARS

Photo on page 5

Approximate size: 42 x 58"

2" squares, 6" blocks

Use 42-45"-wide fabric. When strips appear in the cutting list, cut crossgrain strips (selvage to selvage).

YARDAGE

Borders & More	1501-054 black & white	3 yd
Borders & More	1501-044 blue checkerboard	1¼ yd
Bright prints	⅛ yd each of 19 or more	
Border 1	½ yd yellow	
Border 2 corners	⅙ yd white	
Binding	½ yd fuchsia	
Backing	2⅞ yd	
Batting	46 x 62"	

CUTTING

NOTE: Add ¼" seam allowance on all pieces cut from Borders & More fabric.

Borders & More - black & white

5 star blocks

2 pieces double sawtooth 26 large triangle units long

2 pieces double sawtooth 18 large triangle units long

Borders & More - blue checkerboard

5 star blocks

*10 pieces checkerboard 1 by 5 squares

*10 pieces checkerboard 1 by 6 squares

*Cut from inside & outside rows, using center row for seam allowances

Bright prints	294 squares 2½"
Border 1	5 strips 2½"
Border 2 corners	4 squares 3½"
Binding	6 strips 2¼"

DIRECTIONS

Use ¼" seam allowance unless otherwise noted.

1. BLOCKS: Make 10 blocks as shown using stars and checkerboard pieces. Press.

2. ASSEMBLE: Stitch squares into sections as shown. Stitch sections of squares and star blocks into horizontal rows as shown. Stitch rows together. Press.

3. BORDER 1: Measure length of quilt. Piece border strips to the measured length and stitch to sides of quilt. Repeat at top and bottom. Press.

4. BORDER 2: Spread quilt top on floor and place 26-triangle Border 3 pieces close to sides of

1.

2.

Continued on page 12.

4

See other color ideas on page 12.

NOTE: Star blocks in the quilt in this photo are made from 3 Borders & More fabrics:
Style #1500 Pattern #004, Style #1501 Pattern #044, Style #1501 Pattern #054.
Diagram and directions on page 4 use only Style #1501 Pattern #044 & Style #1501 Pattern #054.

FACETS OF COLOR

Photo on page 7

Approximate size: 44 x 59″   7½″ blocks

Use 42-45″-wide fabric. When strips appear in the cutting list, cut crossgrain strips (selvage to selvage).

NOTE: Our model is made of scraps, approximately 35 brights were used (yellow, orange, blue, teal, periwinkle, purple, lime, & fuchsia). The bright print yardage in the chart below could be ¼ yard each of the 8 colors named above and would make a similar quilt.

YARDAGE

Borders & More 1501-044
  blue checkerboard/teal triangles 3 yd

Bright prints	¼ yd each of 8 or more
Black	1⅝ yd
Blue	⅙ yd
Binding	½ yd
Backing	3 yd
Batting	48 x 63″

CUTTING

NOTE: Add ¼″ seam allowance on all pieces cut from Borders & More fabric.

Borders & More fabric:
  2 pieces teal double triangles 48″ long
  2 pieces teal double triangles 34″ long
  2 pieces blue checkerboard 55″ long - include black & purple ¼″ stripes PLUS seam allowance on either side
  2 pieces blue checkerboard 40″ long - include black & purple ¼″ stripes PLUS seam allowance on either side

Blocks	bright prints	*84 squares 3⅜″
		24 squares 3″
	black	*84 squares 3⅜″
		24 squares 3″
Border 1	black	5 strips 2⅝″
		4 squares 4″
Border 2	blue	4 squares 4⅛″
Binding		6 strips 2¼″

*Cut these squares in HALF diagonally.

DIRECTIONS

Use ¼″ seam allowance unless otherwise noted.

1. BLOCKS: Make 24 blocks using fabrics as desired. Quilt in photo has 2-4 blocks made of each color. A different colored triangle is placed in the center of each block. Press.

2. ASSEMBLE: Stitch blocks into 6 rows of 4, rotating as shown. Stitch rows together. Press.

3. BORDER 1: Stitch 2⅝″ black pieces end to end. Cut into 2 pieces 48″ long and 2 pieces 34″ long. Stitch to teal triangle pieces. Press.

1. Make 6
    Make 1

   Make 24

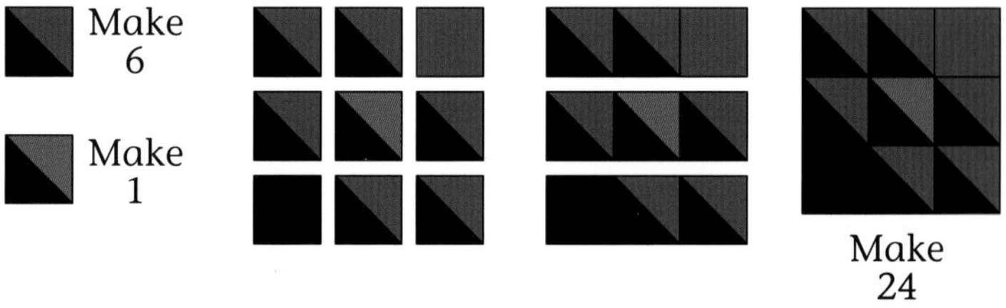

2.

Continued on page 13.

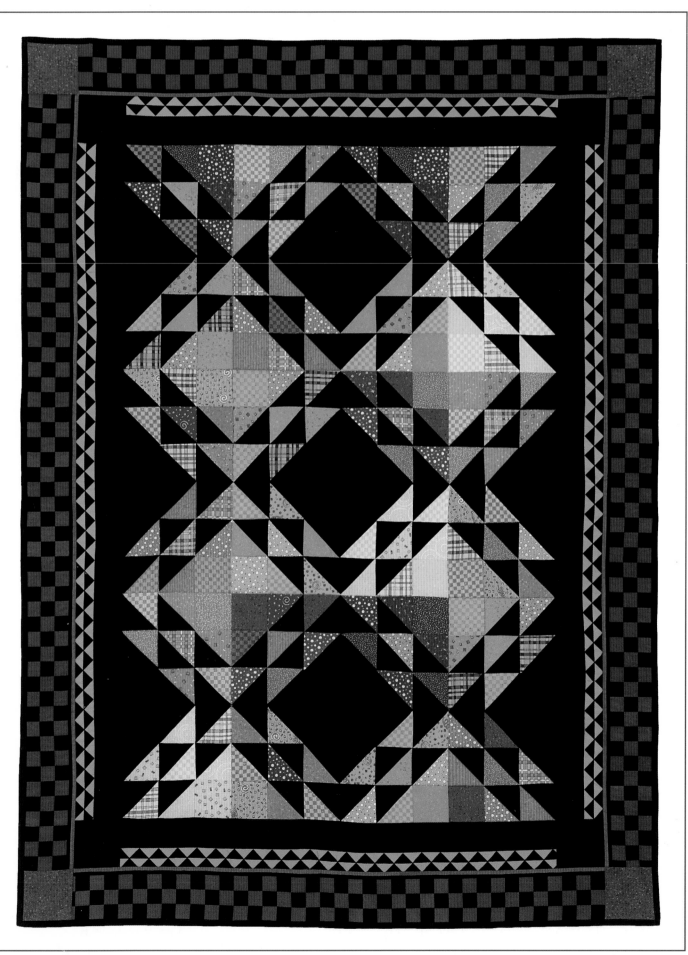

See other color ideas on page 13.

BASICALLY BORDERS

Photo on page 9

Approximate size: 56 x 70"

Use 42-45"-wide fabric. When strips appear in the
cutting list, cut crossgrain strips (selvage to selvage).

YARDAGE

Borders & More
  1501-703 - pastel   3 yd
Border   1½ yd
Vine   ¼ yd green
Leaves   ⅛ yd each of 4 or more fabrics
Flowers   ⅙ yd each of 4 or more fabrics
Binding   ⅝ yd
Backing   3¾ yd
Batting   62 x 76"

CUTTING

Borders & More   2 pieces 42½" long, centering
                      stars from end to end, &
                      starting with the same star
                      at the left
Border   6 strips 7½"
Appliques   see patterns on page 15
Binding   7 strips 2¼"

DIRECTIONS

Use ¼" seam allowance unless otherwise noted.

1. CENTER PANEL:

   Panel 1: Trim upper edge to leave ¼" seam
   allowance (yellow) beyond the white triangles.
   Trim lower edge to leave ¼" seam allowance
   below the checkerboard (white).

   Panel 2: Trim upper edge to leave ½" of yellow
   beyond the white triangles. Trim lower edge to
   leave ¼" seam allowance below the yellow and
   white triangles (yellow).

   Stitch Panel 2 to lower edge of Panel 1. Press.

2. BORDER: Measure length of quilt. Piece border
   strips to the measured length and stitch to
   sides of quilt. Repeat at top and bottom. Press.

3. APPLIQUE: Applique vines and flowers to
   border. See page 15 for vine segment place-
   ment diagram. Cover ends of vines with
   flowers and leaves.

4. LAYERING & QUILTING: Piece backing horizontally to same size as batting. Layer and
   quilt as desired. Trim backing and batting
   even with top.

5. BINDING: Stitch binding strips together end to
   end. Press in half lengthwise, wrong sides
   together. Bind quilt using ¼" seam allowance.

Continued on page 14.

1.

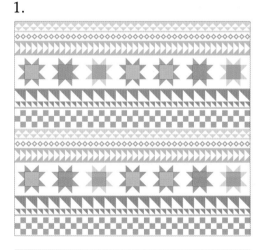

Panel 1

Panel 2

2.

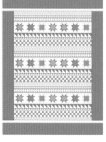

See other color ideas on page 14.

ROW BY ROW

Photo on page 11

Approximate size: 42×58″

Use 42-45″-wide fabric. When strips appear in the cutting list, cut crossgrain strips (selvage to selvage).

YARDAGE

Borders & More
  1501-054 - black & white   1½ yd
Reds & blues   ¼ yd each of 10 fabrics
Binding   ½ yd
Backing   2⅞ yd
Batting   46×62″

CUTTING

Borders & More
  1 piece of each border unit 42″ long, centering design elements from end to end
  checkerboard, flying geese, stars, sawtooth, diamonds/triangles

Reds & blues   1 strip 5½×42″ of 2 of the blues for top & bottom
                1 strip 4½×42″ of each remaining fabric

Binding   6 strips 2¼″

DIRECTIONS

Use ¼″ seam allowance unless otherwise noted.

1. CENTER PANEL: Arrange rows as shown in diagram, placing 5½″ strips at top and bottom. Stitch. Press. Trim sides to square up.

2. LAYERING & QUILTING: Piece backing horizontally to same size as batting. Layer and quilt as desired. Trim backing and batting even with top.

3. BINDING: Stitch binding strips together end to end. Press in half lengthwise, wrong sides together. Bind quilt using ¼″ seam allowance.

Christmas Variation

Juvenile Variation

For the variations above, cut a novelty stripe fabric into strips of various widths. Add pieces of Borders & More and other coordinated prints as needed to make quilt approximately 58″ long.

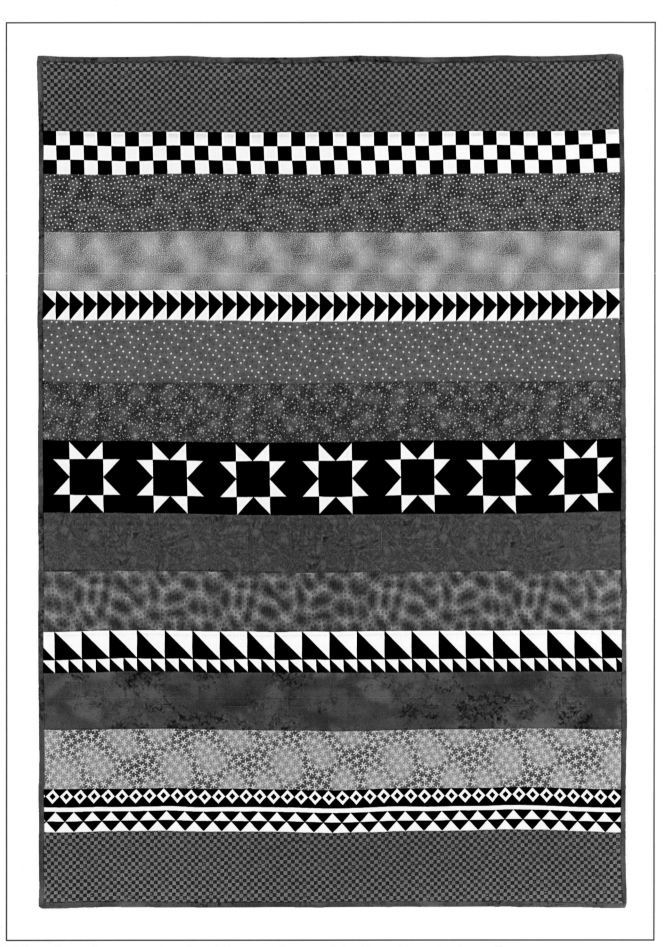

This quilt makes up so fast that it is great for a quick gift or for a charity quilt.

SPRINKLING OF STARS

Continued from page 4.

quilt. If borders are a bit short, cut 3½"
coping strips of white fabric the width
needed and stitch them to each end of
each side border. See Coping Strips,
page 3. If border is a bit long, trim each
end, dividing the difference. See
Dividing Design Elements, page 3.
Stitch side borders to quilt. Repeat the
fitting process at top and bottom of
quilt with remaining border pieces,
stitch corner squares to border pieces,
and stitch borders to quilt. Press.

5. LAYERING & QUILTING: Piece backing
   horizontally to same size as batting.
   Layer and quilt as desired. Trim backing
   and batting even with top.

6. BINDING: Stitch binding strips together
   end to end. Press in half lengthwise,
   wrong sides together. Bind quilt using
   ¼" seam allowance.

4.

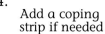

Add a coping
strip if needed

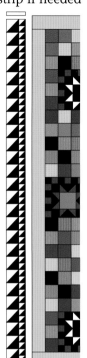

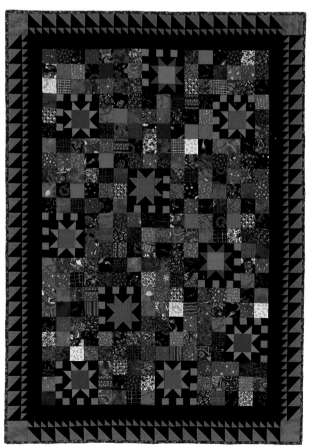

Christmas variation of Sprinkling of Stars
Style #1600 Pattern #084

Pastel variation of Sprinkling of Stars
Style #1501 Pattern #703

FACETS OF COLOR

Continued from page 6.

Spread quilt top on floor and place 48″ border pieces close to sides of quilt. Trim borders to fit quilt, dividing pattern from end to end. See Dividing Design elements, page 3. Stitch to sides of quilt. Repeat fitting process at top and bottom of quilt using remaining border pieces, stitch black corner squares to ends of border pieces, and stitch borders to quilt. Press.

4. BORDER 2: Spread quilt top on floor and place 55″ blue checkerboard pieces close to the sides of the quilt. Trim borders to fit quilt, dividing pattern from end to end. See Dividing Design elements, page 3. Stitch side borders to quilt, purple stripe to inside. Repeat

3.

4.

fitting process at top and bottom of quilt, stitch blue corner squares to ends of printed border pieces, and stitch borders to quilt. Press.

5. LAYERING & QUILTING: Piece backing horizontally to same size as batting. Layer and quilt

as desired. Trim backing and batting even with top.

6. BINDING: Stitch binding strips together end to end. Press in half lengthwise, wrong sides together. Bind quilt using ¼″ seam allowance.

Pastel variation of Facets of Color
Style #1501 Pattern #703

Patriotic variation of Facets of Color
Style #1502 Pattern #001

Christmas variation of Basically Borders.
Style #1600 Pattern #084. Holly patterns on page 15.

Patriotic variation of Basically Borders.
Style #1502 Pattern #001. Star patterns on page 15.

MORE BORDER IDEAS

An easy finish is to end borders bluntly so no corner units have to be made. This also allows the use of borders of different widths. Simply extend top and bottom borders the full width of the quilt.

Use the stars as they come on the yardage with the black area between them as part of the design of the border. Use cornerstones to turn corners.

The star blocks can be used as cornerstones for borders. Extend the width of the other borders to the size of the star block by using a coordinating fabric.

Star blocks can be cut apart and used as individual blocks so the star points meet and the colors of the stars can be arranged as desired.

Cut 30

1½"

Place 7 vine segments on top border and 4 on each side border. Repeat at bottom. Overlap and trim vine segments at corners as needed.

Patterns are for fusible web applique.

Cut 4 (lge. flowers)

FLOWERS

Cut 14   Cut 14

Cut 4 (lge. flowers)

FLOWERS

Cut 4 (lge. flowers)

Cut 8 (small flowers)

Cut 8 (small flowers)

PATRIOTIC
Cut 22

Cut 4

Cut 8

FLOWERS PATRIOTIC

Cut 58

Cut 10 Leaves
Cut 8 leaves reversed

Cut 8 Vine Segments

CHRISTMAS

Use one or two fabrics per leaf.

Cut 8

Cut 14

15

BORDERS & MORE FABRICS

At press time, these are the Borders & More fabrics that are available.
Check your local fabric store for the current versions.

Style #1501 Pattern #054 Style #1500 Pattern #004 Style #1501 Pattern #044

Style #1501 Pattern #703 Style #1600 Pattern #084 Style #1502 Pattern #001

Let your creativity soar
with Borders & More!